MARTIAL LEADERSHIP

Discover and unleash your inner warrior to emerge as the undisputed leader everywhere

Ramanathan J

Copyright © 2019 by Ramanathan J. All Rights Reserved.

All rights reserved. No part of this book may be reproduced in any form or by any electronic or mechanical means including information storage and retrieval systems, without permission in writing from the author. The only exception is by a reviewer, who may quote short excerpts in a review.

Cover designed by Ramanathan J

CONTENTS

Introduction: 2
External environment and its impact 14
Attributes of martial leadership 25
Identify an adversary 26
Vision 32
Purpose 38
Strategy 42
Conclusion 52

INTRODUCTION:

You are fighting a war. You have always been in a conflict since you were born. Your adversaries may have changed but you would have been on the frontlines in one battlefield or the other.

As an infant, you fought for attention from your parents. You also fought against your vulnerabilities and weakness as an infant. You were exposed to a new environment when you were a kid and you were sent to the school for the first time. You could have found this environment to be harsh. You would have also met and dealt with some of your schoolmates who were nasty or toxic.

You may not have realized then as a kid but even some of your relatives would not have taken a liking for you when you went to meet them with your parents. You would have found some of their comments to be snarky.

As you grew up, your battles became more intense and your battlefield became bigger. As you entered college, you faced intense competition to achieve academic excellence. You fought to become a part of one group or the other in college in order to achieve social camaraderie.

Meanwhile, when you entered the corporate world to earn a professional career, you would have realized that the nature of war has changed significantly. Competition for professional success is far more intense and relentless than competition for academic excellence. The stakes are now higher. Professional success could lead to higher salary , better designation, more benefits and a higher position in the hierarchy.

Your colleagues at your workplace will watch your every move with intense focus. Your colleagues will consider you a staunch competitor even though they may mask their ambition against you with fake masks of friendliness and humility.

Your boss or your superiors will be equally wary of your commitment and dedication. They will find in you a contender who could overthrow them or even surpass them in the quest for climbing the corporate ladder and for achieving greater rewards. Newcomers who will join the organization after you will also consider you an eventual competitor. They might report to you or will learn the tools of the trade from you but their dedication and their loyalty will be towards their self-interests.

You will constantly face adversaries and hostilities in your external environment as you work towards realizing your ambitions or achieving your goals. Your battle with your competitors could be overt or it could be more covert in nature. You will be fighting more intense battles as you set higher goals for yourself.

You are also fighting another war whose battle lines drawn within you. You are constantly fighting your own inadequacies and weaknesses that limit you in your quest towards excellence. You might have gained victory over some of your limitations so far, others could be more formidable and so deeply entrenched within you that you may have been battling them for several years. Martial leadership is one quality that can equip you with the right mindset to fight your external as well as internal battles.

Why Martial Leadership?

We have heard of the term martial spirit or fighting spirit. Some individuals are known to have tremendous fighting spirit and an ability to take on any challenge. These individuals are ready for competing in difficult scenarios and are equally willing to accomplish complex tasks.

Others are laid back or easy going by nature. These individuals are not too keen to engage in planning or goal setting. Instead, they react to scenarios and prefer a simple approach towards their various priorities.

Now you may wonder as to what is the difference between martial spirit and martial leadership. Spirit implies an inherent attribute or a characteristic in an individual. A person could be born with a martial spirit or he/she could nurture and develop this quality over a period of time. You could rely on your inherent martial spirit as a preferred or a primary response to challenges or goals.

Leadership indicates an ability to take command or charge of ourselves as well as the external scenarios. Leadership ability can equip an individual with courage, conviction and clarity to take on any task or objective.

Leadership qualities in an individual makes him/her the rallying point for others who might be working in the same organization or who are living in the same society, city or community. Leaders are able to look beyond the obvious and can foresee emerging trends. Leaders can be decisive in driving change.

Martial leadership takes this concept further by imbibing a strategic quality to individuals. Martial leadership enables you to remain centered and calm while you are in the middle of any battlefield. Martial leadership empowers you to strategize and evaluate various possibilities while working towards any objective. You can charge towards your objectives and be on the offensive when you apply the principles of martial leadership.

You may now wonder whether there is too much of a difference between martial spirit and martial leadership. You may think that if you apply your fighting spirit while completing most of the challenges or while achieving many of your goals, you will eventually develop a martial leadership quality.

This could be possible but we may not know whether we will be able to progress towards the leadership ability. We might even be trapped in a fighting spirit mindset. We may use this mindset to automatically respond to new objectives like a muscle memory.

The difference between martial spirit and martial leadership is similar to the difference between a frontline soldier and an army general. A frontline soldier responds to the adversaries who are facing him. He relies on tactics and quick reaction time to deal with the hostilities and march further towards his objectives on the battlefield.

On the other hand, an army general has a strategic overview of the entire battlefield. The general commands over numerous personnel and resources. His stakes are higher and his decisions could prove to be significant for the entire army and the war effort. Thus, the general relies more on developing a brilliant strategy to achieve the overall goals. He uses the information that is available to him and deploys his resources and his personnel accordingly. The general needs leadership ability to command his personnel, to obtain clarity on the battlefield and to define the strategy and objectives of the entire war effort.

You now know the subtle difference between a martial spirit and a martial leadership mindset. Do you wish to rely solely on your martial spirit and be a frontline soldier who constantly reacts to external environment? Or do you seek to develop your martial leadership quality and take charge of the entire battlefield?

Martial leadership will allow you to look at the entire external environment with better clarity. You will be able to define your most important objectives and the reasons for pursuing them. Martial leadership will empower you to develop a strategic response while marching towards your objectives. Finally, you will be able to conserve your precious energy and resources by deciding which projects or objectives are worth to focus upon.

Martial leadership quality will determine how far you can go to achieve your goals. This quality will determine whether you will be overwhelmed by the external environment or whether you will conquer one battlefield after another while marching towards achieving your goals.

You can be a soldier who dodges bullets whizzing past him, fires couple of shots at his enemies, throws a grenade or two and then takes cover to escape return fire. Or you can be a general who calls in a heavy artillery strike and obliterates the entire enemy frontline. What resources you have and use depends upon the mindset that you adopt. Your choice between martial spirit or martial leadership will determine your eventual outcome in your war towards excellence.

Cognitive ability as a resource

If you choose to approach your challenges and objectives with a martial leadership mindset, you need to make appropriate use of the resources at your disposal to achieve your goals. Your key resources are your senses, conscious mind and your imagination/creative faculties. You must use these abilities as resources as you face your competition, adversaries or the external environment.

MARTIAL LEADERSHIP

Your senses are some of your most crucial resources or abilities because your senses determine the inputs that your brain or your conscious mind receive. Your sensory inputs play a key role in shaping your thoughts and opinions that eventually impact the outcome of any endeavor you pursue.

Sensory input to outcome process

As we can see in the above figure, sensory inputs start the entire process for thinking and working towards an outcome or a goal. Sensory inputs direct our conscious mind towards an object. This object attracts our focus or our attention. Our focus determines our thoughts. Directed thoughts lead to focused action and this eventually affects the pace with which we work towards our priorities.

For example, let us assume that you are working in an organization whose business is facing a downturn. You have heard rumors that layoffs are imminent and your department could be one of the prime targets for this exercise. You realize that you need to learn new skills quickly so that you can utilize those skills for getting a new career opportunity elsewhere.

However, your smartphone apps also constantly bombard your senses with a barrage of WhatsApp jokes, Facebook status updates and Instagram pictures. Part of your focus and attention is on these trivial social media exchanges. You are now unable to direct your complete focus on learning new career related skills because you are now also thinking about those exotic vacation photos that your friend uploaded on Instagram.

Direct your senses with utmost discretion. Your conscious mind will process your sensory inputs and hence you need to decide whether the new status update on Facebook or the funny forward on WhatsApp is worth your attention. You need to decide whether you must focus your conscious mind on such trivialities or whether you must direct your thoughts and actions working towards a worthy goal or an objective.

Your conscious mind can help you in crucial tasks such as strategic planning, goal setting and decision making. A sharp conscious mind can empower you with better logical reasoning and critical thinking abilities. Deploy your attention and cognitive faculties wisely as you apply a martial leadership mindset towards achieving your goals.

EXTERNAL ENVIRONMENT AND ITS IMPACT

Man is a social animal. Human beings always have a need to belong to a social group or a system for self-preservation. Primeval human beings were a part of tribe who would hunt and protect each other. As societies advanced, mankind formed larger groups or communities to develop and prosper together. These communities took various forms such as kingdoms or nations.

However, once a human being joins a community or becomes a part of society, the larger group does not take care of this person without any pre-conditions. Community or society members are expected to learn and follow certain rules or behaviors. This is to ensure that the community or a group works cohesively towards mutual prosperity and progress.

Society conditions its members in a systematic manner from early on. Society uses a system of rewards and penalties to shape the behavior pattern of its members. Those who follow the traditional path in a society are benefited with stable and secure lives. These members are accepted as cogs that are a part of bigger machine. However, mavericks in a society face uncertainty. They would not be a small cog of a bigger machine. A maverick can either fade into obscurity or can rise to unprecedented greatness.

Tools of external environment and core beliefs

Society uses various tools to shape its member from the start. School, college, workplace and family are some of the most common instruments for crafting an individual's behavior and expectations. These instruments also create some of the most subtle core beliefs within you.

What did you learn when you were in school? Pay attention in class, follow teacher's instructions, do not speak too much or ask too many questions else you will ruffle many feathers. You could remember that on many occasions, your teacher would have reprimanded you for speaking too much with your neighboring friend.

You could also vaguely remember the incident when you did not understand a topic that was taught in the class .When you asked a question about the same to your teacher, you would have faced verbal rebuke from her and you would have become an object of amusement for the entire class.

How did such incidents in school affect your core beliefs? Perhaps you would now think that it is better to stay silent and mind own business instead of networking or socializing with colleagues or coworkers at your workplace. You could also refrain from getting too curious and asking too many questions when you are discussing about a task with your superior.

Are the school incidents and your behavior years later in workplace directly related? There may not be a direct correlation between the two, however, your early years in the school and the events that you experienced there would have cemented a subtle belief in you that it is better to stay silent and to refrain from freely expressing your thoughts.

Similarly, your earlier interactions in the family will also play a major role in establishing certain key beliefs within you. Parental upbringing, interaction with siblings and your relatives also play a major role in shaping your behavior patterns. Like school, family conditions or programs your beliefs from early on.

While many of the beliefs that you have acquired from your interaction with your immediate family could be beneficial for you, you must realize that some of those beliefs may not be work in your favor if you try to adopt a martial leadership mindset.

You must have heard often that you need to get good grades, get into a stable career and then get settled. You may even cherish this inherited wisdom as a core belief. But, if you want to dominate the numerous battlefields, you need to emerge victorious in the countless battles that you are waging in your quest towards excellence and aspirations.

Martial leadership quality does not evolve when you follow the tried and tested method of reacting to the external environment and settling down. Martial leadership requires you to challenge the status quo and go on the offensive to tame the external environment in your favor. Martial leadership enables you to aggressively work towards your goals provided you are not bogged down by a stability and security seeking mindset.

Not many of us are born with an innate quality for martial leadership. Naturally, many of the advice or wisdom we receive are traditional or conformist in nature. You need to introspect and examine your core assumptions that also act as your beliefs. Some of these assumptions could be impeding you from developing a martial leadership quality. These assumptions are like invisible shackles that have tied you down. You need to evaluate these assumptions and let go of some of them, if required.

Emerging from impeding assumptions or beliefs

You may now agree that certain core assumptions or beliefs are driving many of your behavioral patterns. Some of these behavioral patterns could also be hindering your overall development towards developing a martial leadership quality. The question now we face is how we can identify and move on from these impeding core assumptions.

You can use the following framework that I would like to call as the "Convergence Diagram".

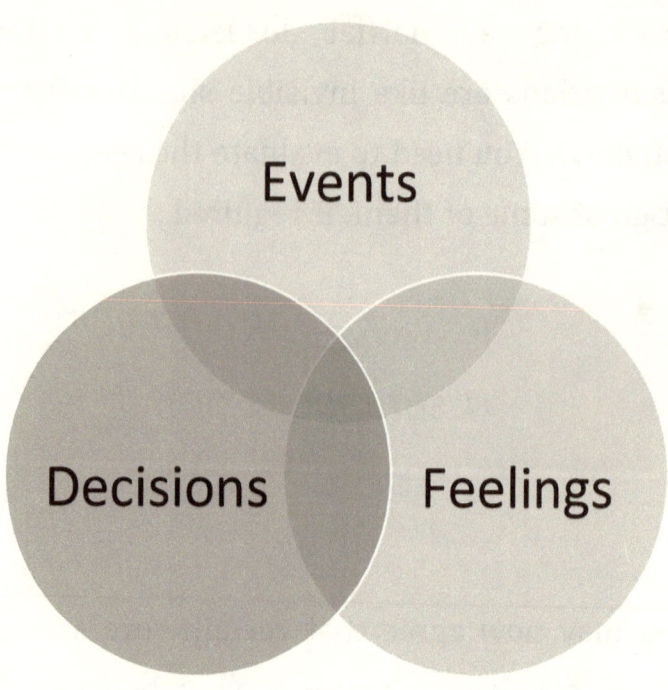

In the above diagram, events represent the key incidents that has happened to you so far. Some of the events could be key such as your college graduation or your first job. Some other events may not seem significant to you at first but you will be able to remember them. For example, you may remember the late night party with your school friends during one summer.

Decisions are those key moments when you faced a couple of choices and you took a decision to choose one of those choices. For example, you could have got admission in many colleges, but you chose one of them. You could have chosen any of the several career choices, yet you selected one of them. You could have got several job offers but you chose one of them.

Feelings represent the third part of the diagram. Feelings determine our reaction to the events or decisions that we faced at various stages. These events or decisions could be related to our external environment but feelings describe our interpretation or meaning. Feelings emerge from our core assumptions or beliefs and could thus point to those areas where we need to work on.

For example, how did you feel when you completed your college graduation? Did you feel excited for the upcoming career prospects? Or did you feel glad that somehow you managed to get a degree? Why did you feel the way you did at those moments? The answer could point you towards those core assumptions that are deeply rooted within you.

Similarly, you could have decided to become a doctor or an accountant. What were your feelings when you were thinking about either of these career options? Did you choose to become a doctor because you were always fascinated by the profession since your childhood? Or did you choose to become an accountant because you wanted a stable and a secure career option? How did you evaluate your career options and arrive at a conclusion?

Our decisions at key stages represent our underlying feelings and core assumptions. Our decisions always include an element of irrationality that emerges from our core beliefs. We need to evaluate our key decisions to understand our priorities and feelings at those stages.

Once you identify your feelings during key events or decisions in your life, you can derive the reasons or assumptions because of which you had those feelings. These assumptions are your core beliefs and they are driving your behavior, thoughts and actions in every endeavor that you pursue.

When you understand your core assumptions, you can evaluate each of them and determine whether these assumptions have benefited you or obstructed you whenever you have worked towards any objective or goal. For example, you may have pursued art in your college days because you would have assumed then that you can learn any new subject if you put in enough effort and dedication. Such core assumptions or beliefs will help in strengthening your martial leadership quality.

Another example could be that you never pursued mathematics major in college because you believed that you were not good with numbers. These core assumptions obstruct your ability to develop martial leadership qualities. The best way to deal with these assumptions is to prove them wrong, repeatedly. If you have believed that you are an introvert, then go out and start socializing. If you have assumed that you are not good in numbers, then start solving number based puzzles every day. Eventually, you will move on from the assumptions that halt your progress towards developing a martial leadership quality. This quality alone will matter a lot to you in your future battles.

ATTRIBUTES OF MARTIAL LEADERSHIP

IDENTIFY AN ADVERSARY

Civilized societies often refrain from supporting open confrontation or hostilities. War mongering nations are isolated in the international community. People look down upon overtly aggressive individuals. Such persons with a confrontational approach find few allies in their workplace and are often required to wage a lonely war against their adversarial coworkers or superiors.

However, you must understand that people secretly harbor resentment and hostile intentions towards those who are inimical to their self-interests. Many individuals can quickly size people up and classify them in an us versus them framework. You must ignore the fake smiles and superficial niceties of those with whom you interact at your workplace. Instead, you must interpret their real intentions.

Many people will pretend to be diplomatic and courteous in order to blend in to the organization or the community to which they belong. However, many of them will not stop from scheming or plotting to achieve what they want.

Your co-workers, colleagues or so-called friends are all competing for the same prize. They will not be too keen to share the rewards with you as a token of goodwill or friendship. You must consider such adversaries as an inherent part of your journey towards achieving your ambitions. A general does not retreat from the battlefield after he confronts enemy army divisions. Instead, he accepts their presence as just a variable to factor in his overall strategy. Similarly, you must identify, classify and deal with your adversaries or competitors in your environment in a dispassionate manner.

Adversary – A concept

We often consider an adversary as an individual or a person. However, adversary need not be a person. An adversary could also be a concept or an idea that we loathe. Our external environment comprise of persons who may be envious of us or those who are resentful towards us. Similarly, our community, organization or society also includes ideas or qualities that we cannot stand.

Maybe you are repulsed by the arrogant behavior of some of your co-workers in your workplace. Maybe you are disgusted by the narcissistic behavior of your former college friends, who cannot stop uploading pictures of their exotic vacations on the social media. Perhaps you may detest your boss, who treats you in a condescending manner every time you discuss a work related idea.

An adversary, which could be an idea or a person, is a guiding star that you can rely upon as you wage a relentless war to accomplish your objectives. An adversary can motivate you and spur you into taking decisive action for turning the odds in your favor. An adversary can infuse a new zeal within you to explore many possibilities or try various strategies to achieve your goals.

Your endeavors or projects will have a new meaning if you seek to accomplish an objective in order to emerge victorious over your adversary. A brand new career opportunity with a significant raise in salary will definitely silence your arrogant former co-workers. An organization wide recognition for you will certainly make your boss think twice henceforth before behaving in a condescending manner with you. You must not consume your resentment towards adversarial individuals or values. Instead, you must channelize your resentment towards your adversaries to accomplish your goals.

Dealing with adversaries

Adversarial values or individuals are a recurring roadblock in your pursuit towards your goals. You will be spending enough of your resources and energy engaging your adversaries in skirmishes instead of working towards your goal unless you identify a strategy for dealing with hostile elements.

The first step in dealing with adversaries is to stop accepting things at face value and analyze the facts to find out the real meaning. This means you are not swayed by the courteous and friendly behavior of your friends and colleagues. You need to judge people by their actions and not by their words. In case of internal adversaries, you have to become self-aware and analyze the core assumptions that are driving your behaviors and key decisions.

The next step is to accept the presence of adversaries and acknowledge that they will impede our progress while we work towards our goals. You must ignore the so-called suggestions or opinions that these adversaries may have about your capabilities or ambitions. You must remember that these adversaries have no stakes in your quest towards achieving your goals. You must realize that no one can judge you better than yourself. Your only aim must be to think beyond your adversaries and work towards your goal.

Once you successfully achieve your objectives, you will prove your adversaries wrong.

As far as adversarial beliefs are concerned, the best way to deal with them is to identify the underlying core assumptions that are inimical to our self-development and act contrary to these assumptions in order to grow beyond them.

VISION

A captain of any ship needs a destination before he sets out for sail. Without a destination, the ship will be soon adrift in the waters and its crew will soon run out of food, water and energy.

Similarly, you cannot wage countless battles in all directions and hope that eventually you will strike gold. You need a north star to direct your plans and actions in a meaningful manner. A vision statement will provide you with the guidance and wisdom on which battles you should fight and which ones you should skip.

A vision statement represents an overarching objective or a goal. A vision statement is like a string that ties a series of projects or activities to achieve one grand goal. If martial leadership is an engine, then a vision statement is the fuel that drives this engine. A vision statement is the big picture that provides a larger context for our actions or endeavors.

A vision statement enables us to look beyond the daily skirmishes and to retain our focus on the grand objective. A compelling vision statement can inspire us to achieve our goals in the most elegant manner. Our vision can guide us to take detours or search for better ways in our quest for excellence. You can determine which projects matter or which tasks are better to skip by focusing on your vision statement and ranking your tasks in the order of relative importance towards achieving your greater goals.

Crafting a vision statement

Some individuals have an immense clarity of the bigger picture from very early on. They can articulate about how their actions are steps taken towards a greater objective. It is as if a sense of destiny drives such individuals towards a grand ambition.

You may now wonder as to how an individual, who does not have such an appealing vision statement from the beginning, can identify and design one. To start with, introspect and figure out if you constantly gravitate towards one picture or snapshot that represents what you aspire. For example, you may constantly think of driving a luxury car or living in a fancy apartment.

You now need to identify these disparate ambitions and combine them to form one compelling vision statement. Thus, you can articulate your vision statement as follows- I am driving a luxury car from my fancy apartment that is located on neighborhood XYZ. I am driving to work at company A, where I am the Vice President of marketing.

You need to be particularly aware of not settling down with a vague or generic vision statement. Instead, your vision statement should be clear up to the most fine details. Your vision statement should be descriptive and visually appealing. Finally, your vision statement should inspire and motivate you to work towards executing your plans with zeal.

For example, you want to achieve success in your professional career is a vague and generic vision statement. This statement is bland and does not inspire you to seek new strategies or to work towards your goal with aggression.

Now consider this another example- You want to become the senior vice president of marketing in your company. You want to occupy that corner office which overlooks the picturesque location. You want to lead a team of 20 professionals and generate a business of more than 30 million dollars annually. This vision statement is inspiring and also comprise of finer details.

Tools for creating vision statement

You can use traditional techniques for creating your own vision statement. Instead of restricting your vision statement to just one line or couple of statements, you can become more creative to depict your vision statement. For example, you can take a blank canvas as well as couple of magazines and newspapers. You can cut out key images and words that relate to your vision statement. You can then make a visual collage of these images and words by pasting them on your empty canvas. For example, if your vision statement includes driving a yellow sports car and staying in a beach side apartment, you can search your newspaper and magazine collections for images related to cars or luxurious apartments. You can cut out these images and paste them in clusters or groups on your canvas. Each group or cluster will represent one aspect of your vision.

You can also purchase vision board kits such as FaberCastell vision board kit, Magnificent vision board kit or Craftivity Dare to Dream board craft kit from online shopping sites to create your vision statement. You can create your vision statements using these kits or you can use a simple canvas and collage of newspaper pictures. You can use this vision statement canvas into visualize your ambitions by placing it at a convenient location in your home.

PURPOSE

A man always has a reason to fulfill by achieving any goal or objective. This reason is subtle, emotional and visceral in nature. This reason is not related to the external or the materialistic aspect of any goal or objective. Instead, this reason is more personal to an individual.

You can label this deeper reason behind any goal as purpose. Purpose answers the question why behind any activity or project. You may have an aspiration to start your own business instead of continuing with your current job. When you ask yourself why do you want this for the first time, you will get an initial answer that addresses the material benefits of pursuing a goal. Thus, you could say that running your own business could give you an opportunity to work for yourself and to earn more money. You could say that although the risks of running your own business is high, the rewards could also be more.

When you ask yourself the question why again, you would uncover a different reason for working towards a goal. For instance, when you ask yourself again why do you want to run your own business instead of working in an organization as an employee, you might answer that you would like to work your own hours and set your own rules. You would uncover an altogether different reason or perspective for pursuing a goal or an ambition. You need to keep going by repeatedly asking yourself why you need to pursue a goal.

Thus, if you again ask yourself why you want to run your own business instead of working in your current organization, you may finally realize that you cherish independence and that you want to explore the whole process of setting and achieving goals for yourself.

Purpose is always emotional in nature. Purpose transcends material benefits and connects to a more nobler and human reason. Many artists would not say that they have painted a master piece only to earn more money at an auction. Instead, these artists would say that they have painted their creative inspiration on the canvas.

Similarly, many people who join the military would say that they are doing so to serve and safeguard their country. Salary and stable career are nothing more than additional benefits for such individuals. Purpose would give us a more personal and human reason to work towards a goal instead of merely aspiring for material gains.

Martial leadership quality needs purpose to continue to work towards a vision. Purpose defines why we need to change the status quo and aspire for more. For example, you may aspire to become the senior vice president of marketing. Now if you ask yourself why you want this, you may initially answer that the new designation would mean higher salary and better perks. But then you may wonder what is wrong with the current designation and salary. After all, you could be earning a decent salary and could be successful in your current role. Purpose will provide you with a deeper reason for pursuing a goal. Perhaps you like to work with people while working towards a common goal. Maybe you have a natural ability for leadership and you would like to use this ability to lead a team. Maybe you like to interact with people and help them in solving their problems. Repeatedly ask yourself why you want to achieve a goal. You would soon identify a more human and emotional reason or purpose for your goal.

STRATEGY

The term strategy is derived from the Greek word "strategos" which means "the art of the general". Strategy could be defined as the process to identify various courses of actions to achieve long term goals and the allocation of resources to complete these actions. Thus, strategy as a discipline has evolved from various military warfare doctrines. Senior leadership in organizations consider strategy planning one of their key activities.

You should consider strategy a key component of setting and achieving goals. Strategy planning will enable you to define priorities and allocate your resources. You can use strategy planning to define the broad path or measures that you will take while you work towards your goals.

Your initial strategy planning can be restricted to a broad level and need not focus on finer details. Once you have identified all the key stages that would be required for achieving your overall goal, you can list out the detailed tasks for each of the stages in subsequent planning sessions.

For example, suppose an army general wants to capture an enemy city during a military campaign. He receives information from his intelligence assets that the enemy has couple of garrisons and well defended facilities in the city. The general now has to prepare the initial strategy for capturing the enemy city by effectively using his resources. He can call in an air strike on key enemy targets in the city, then send special forces to swiftly take down any remaining resistance and finally deploy his infantry division to capture the enemy city. The general could also launch cruise missile strikes on all enemy locations in the city and then just deploy a larger contingent of special forces to capture the city. Initial strategy planning identifies such broad measures or steps for achieving the primary objective.

Once you have identified the broad series of measures as a part of your overall strategy planning, you can fill in the finer details or tasks for each of these measures in your subsequent planning sessions.

For instance, suppose the military general in our example decides to launch air strike, then send special forces and finally deploy infantry division to capture the enemy city as the overall strategy, he can figure out the minute details in later stages. So in the subsequent planning sessions, the general can analyze and decide on the time to be taken for executing each stage, the number of jets required for the air strike, the number of special forces and infantry division troops required in later stages and so on.

Strategy planning enables you to judiciously deploy the resources that are available with you. Effective strategy planning can prevent excess of a trial and error process to see what works and what doesn't. We can visualize the possibility of success with each set of broad measures and fine tune our overall planning before we use our resources for any project or goal.

Strategy and resources

You may think that you can tirelessly work on any objective. You could believe that you can accomplish complex tasks with limitless will power. You could also believe that determination and grit will be sufficient to explore various possibilities and to see what works.

However, you must remember one fact that is applicable for every human being. You have finite will power and energy reserves. You use your conscious mind and cognitive faculties for a variety of tasks on any given day. You exhaust your limited energy reserves and will power every time you apply your cognitive faculties for any task. Your mind eventually hits a roadblock when you completely run out of your energy reserves.

You may wonder that you do not work on any task non-stop and that you get enough time for rest and recreation every day. You could think that why would you run out of energy reserves or will power on a daily basis while working on a specific task. The answer to this question is in two other abilities that are present in any individual. One is morale and the other one is inner momentum.

Morale motivates and inspires us to continue to work on a task however complex or difficult it may seem. Morale empowers us to strive for a goal even though the odds may seem to be against our favor. We can sustain our morale by continuing to make visible progress towards any goal, however little it may seem. Hence, morale is your most important asset which you must conserve and protect at all costs.

Inner momentum is our ability to improve our efficiency by steadily working on an activity over a period. We are able to master the finer details or intricacies of any task once we work on it for a sustained duration. Our ability as well as our confidence to accomplish the task steadily improves. Inner momentum propels us to take on the next challenging task once we complete the current one.

If you are unable to achieve breakthrough soon while working on an objective, your morale and inner momentum will be affected. You may try various approaches to accomplish a goal and could sustain setbacks in some of them. You will gradually lack enough morale and inner momentum to work on the objective again. You will need more will power just to motivate yourself to start working on the task. Soon, you will be disinterested even to think about the objective.

Morale and inner momentum are intricately linked to the willpower that we derive for any task. The extent of willpower that we require for completing any task is directly dependent upon the morale and inner momentum that we have built up so far for the task. For example, you may have practiced how to play tennis for hundreds of hours. If your friend now invites you to a game of tennis, you will be able to play the game with ease. This is because you have built up your morale and momentum for tennis by practicing how to play the game for many hours. Thus, you do not need enough willpower to play the game.

An effective strategy will ensure that you channelize your will power, morale and inner momentum effectively. You would have explored various possibilities and options for your solution. Hence, you will be able to zero in on the most feasible solution for your objective quickly. An effective strategy will enable you to identify constraints and opportunities that are available in the environment while you work towards your goals.

An effective tool for strategy planning

Although mind map is widely used for creative brainstorming and idea generation activities, you can use this tool as an effective platform for strategy planning exercise as well. You can use your imagination and creative skills to design a compelling mind map. This mind map will act as a single snapshot that would summarize your strategic options or measures required to achieve a goal.

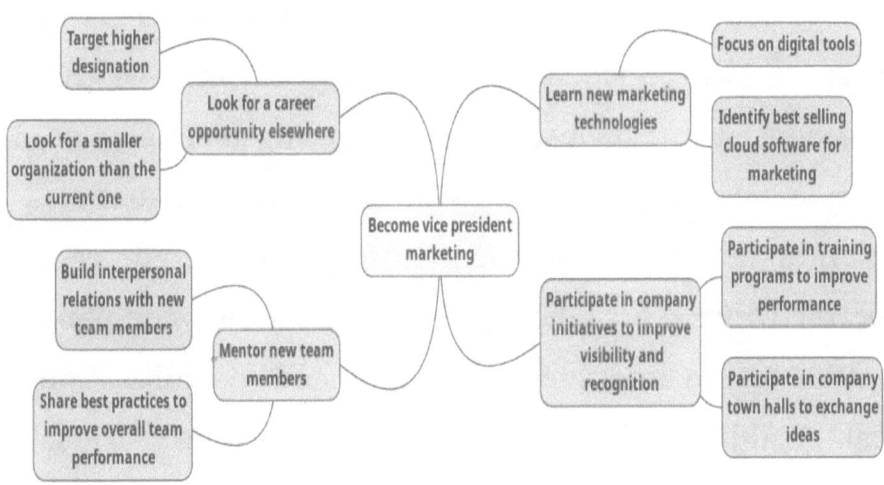

The above image is a basic mind map that you can create with an online tool called as Mindmup. The core objective or idea is located in the center of the mind map. You can then connect various nodes to this core objective. These nodes could represent the possible measures or options that you could utilize to achieve the core objective.

In the above example, the core node or objective is to become vice president of marketing. To achieve this objective, you can learn new marketing technologies, join a new organization with a higher designation, mentor new team members to improve overall team performance or participate in more company initiatives to improve recognition and visibility. You can highlight these possible strategies as various nodes in your mind map. You can apply any of these strategies to achieve your core objective. You can also expand any of these nodes further if you wish to analyze a strategic option in further detail.

These nodes could further be connected to child nodes that can further explore a specific option mentioned in the parent node. In this way, you can extend the mind map or any of its nodes up to as much finer detail as you require. A mind map is a visual summary and hence you can quickly review any of the options that you have identified so far for accomplishing an objective. You can highlight all strategic options that you have figured out so far in the mind map. You can then review these options or expand them further if required. In this way, you can expand this mind map to illustrate all strategic options in one visual snapshot.

CONCLUSION

Martial leadership is a mindset. While everyone possesses a fighting spirit to some extent, martial leadership elevates this approach to a higher level. Martial leadership enables you to stop reacting to external environment and instead take control of the battlefield that lies ahead of you.

You can identify an adversary person or a value and then use that adversary as your inspiration to change the status quo. You can utilize your inherent martial leadership quality to introspect and evaluate your core assumptions that have transformed into your core beliefs over the years. You can analyze these assumptions and move on from those who impede your development or progress.

A compelling vision statement backed by an appealing purpose will inspire you to wage relentless battles for a worthy cause. An effective strategy would ensure that you explore various measures to achieve your objective and that you dedicate your resources to the most feasible approach or solution.

You can achieve excellence in a martial leadership quality by considering your journey towards accomplishing your vision as a war. You will then consider every endeavor or project of yours as an individual battle. Every such battle that you engage in will gradually sharpen your martial leadership skills. You will eventually gain enough expertise to execute your projects with decisiveness, clarity and conviction.

www.ingramcontent.com/pod-product-compliance
Lightning Source LLC
Chambersburg PA
CBHW030734180526
45157CB00008BA/3166